Andrew Lang

Grass of Parnassus : rhymes old and new

Andrew Lang
Grass of Parnassus : rhymes old and new
ISBN/EAN: 9783337261146

Printed in Europe, USA, Canada, Australia, Japan

Cover: Foto ©Thomas Meinert / pixelio.de

More available books at **www.hansebooks.com**

GRASS OF PARNASSUS

GRASS OF PARNASSUS

RHYMES OLD AND NEW

BY ANDREW LANG

LONDON
LONGMANS, GREEN, AND CO.
AND NEW YORK: 15 EAST 16th STREET
1888

PRINTED BY
SPOTTISWOODE AND CO., NEW-STREET SQUARE
LONDON

CONTENTS

DEEDS OF MEN

	PAGE
SEEKERS FOR A CITY	3
THE WHITE PACHA	6
MIDNIGHT, JANUARY 25, 1886	8
ADVANCE, AUSTRALIA	9
COLONEL BURNABY	11
MELVILLE AND COGHILL	12

RHODOCLEIA

TO RHODOCLEIA	15

AVE

CLEVEDON CHURCH	21
*TWILIGHT ON TWEED	23
*METEMPSYCHOSIS	25
*LOST IN HADES	26
*A STAR IN THE NIGHT	27
*A SUNSET ON YARROW	28
ANOTHER WAY	29

*HESPEROTHEN

	PAGE
THE SEEKERS FOR PHÆACIA	33
A SONG OF PHÆACIA	35
THE DEPARTURE FROM PHÆACIA	37
A BALLAD OF DEPARTURE	39
THEY HEAR THE SIRENS FOR THE SECOND TIME	40
CIRCE'S ISLE REVISITED	42
THE LIMIT OF LANDS	44

VERSES

MARTIAL IN TOWN	49
APRIL ON TWEED	51
TIRED OF TOWNS	53
SCYTHE SONG	55
PEN AND INK	56
A DREAM	58
THE SINGING ROSE	59
A REVIEW IN RHYME	62
*COLINETTE	63
*A SUNSET OF WATTEAU	65
*NIGHTINGALE WEATHER	67
*LOVE AND WISDOM	69
*GOOD-BYE	71
*AN OLD PRAYER	73
*A LA BELLE HÉLÈNE	74
*SYLVIE ET AURÉLIE	76
*A LOST PATH	78
*THE SHADE OF HELEN	79

SONNETS

	PAGE
SHE	83
HERODOTUS IN EGYPT	84
*GÉRARD DE NERVAL	85
*RONSARD	86
*LOVE'S MIRACLE	87
*DREAMS	88
*TWO SONNETS OF THE SIRENS	89

TRANSLATIONS

*HYMN TO THE WINDS	93
*MOONLIGHT	94
*THE GRAVE AND THE ROSE	95
*A VOW TO HEAVENLY VENUS	96
*OF HIS LADY'S OLD AGE	97
*SHADOWS OF HIS LADY	98
*APRIL	99
*AN OLD TUNE	103
*OLD LOVES	104
*A LADY OF HIGH DEGREE	106
*IANNOULA	108
*THE MILK WHITE DOE	109
HELIODORE	112
THE PROPHET	113
LAIS	114
CLEARISTA	115
THE FISHERMAN'S TOMB	116
OF HIS DEATH	117

	PAGE
Rhodope	118
To a Girl	119
To the Ships	120
A Late Convert	121
The Limit of Life	122
To Daniel Elzevir	123

THE LAST CHANCE

The Last Chance	127

GRASS OF PARNASSUS.

PALE star that by the lochs of Galloway,
    In wet green places 'twixt the depth and height
Dost keep thine hour while Autumn ebbs away,
    When now the moors have doffed the heather bright,
    Grass of Parnassus, flower of my delight,
How gladly with the unpermitted bay—
Garlands not mine, and leaves that not decay—
    How gladly would I twine thee if I might!

The bays are out of reach! But far below
    The peaks forbidden of the Muses' Hill,
Grass of Parnassus, thy returning snow
    Between September and October chill
Doth speak to me of Autumns long ago,
    And these kind faces that are with me still.

MANY of the verses and translations in this volume were published first in *Ballads and Lyrics of Old France* (1872). Though very sensible that they have the demerits of imitative and even of undergraduate rhyme, I print them again because people I like have liked them. The rest are of different dates, and lack (though doubtless they need) the excuse of having been written, like some of the earlier pieces, during College Lectures. I would gladly have added to this volume what other more or less serious rhymes I have written, but circumstances over which I have no control have bound them up with *Ballades*, and other toys of that sort.

It may be as well to repeat in prose, what has already been said in verse, that Grass of Parnassus, the pretty Autumn flower, grows in the marshes at the foot of the Muses' Hill, and other hills, not at the top by any means.

Several of the versions from the Greek Anthology have been published in the *Fortnightly Review*, and the sonnet on Colonel Burnaby appeared in *Punch*. These, with pieces from other serials, are reprinted by the courteous permission of the Editors.

The verses that were published in *Ballades and Lyrics*, and in *Ballades and Verses Vain* (Charles Scribner's Sons, New York), are marked in the contents with an asterisk.

TO
E. M. S.

Primâ dicta mihi, summâ dicenda Camenâ.

The 'years will pass, and hearts will range,
You conquer Time, and Care, and Change.
Though Time doth still delight to shed
The dust on many a younger head;
Though Care, oft coming, hath the guile
From younger lips to steal the smile;
Though Change makes younger hearts wax cold,
And sells new loves for loves of old,
Time, Change, nor Care, hath learned the art
To fleck your hair, to chill your heart,
To touch your tresses with the snow,
To mar your mirth of long ago.
Change, Care, nor Time, while life endure,
Shall spoil our ancient friendship sure,
The love which flows from sacred springs,
In 'old unhappy far-off things,'
From sympathies in grief and joy,
Through all the years of man and boy.

Therefore, to you, the rhymes I strung
When even this 'brindled' head was young
I bring, and later rhymes I bring
That flit upon as weak a wing,
But still for you, for yours, they sing!

DEEDS OF MEN

ἄειδε δ' ἄρα κλέα ἀνδρῶν

TO

COLONEL IAN HAMILTON

To you, who know the face of war,
You, that for England wander far,
You that have seen the Ghazis fly
From English lads not sworn to die,
You that have lain where, deadly chill,
The mist crept o'er the Shameful Hill,
You that have conquered, mile by mile,
The currents of unfriendly Nile,
And cheered the march, and eased the strain
When Politics made valour vain,
Ian, to you, from banks of Ken,
We send our lays of Englishmen!

SEEKERS FOR A CITY.

'Believe me, if that blissful, that beautiful place, were set on a hill visible to all the world, I should long ago have journeyed thither. . . . But the number and variety of the ways! For you know, *There is but one road that leads to Corinth.*'   HERMOTIMUS (Mr. Pater's Version).

'The Poet says, *dear city of Cecrops*, and wilt thou not say, *dear city of Zeus?*'   M. ANTONINUS.

TO Corinth leads one road, you say:
   Is there a Corinth, or a way?
Each bland or blatant preacher hath
His painful or his primrose path,
And not a soul of all of these
But knows the city 'twixt the seas,
Her fair unnumbered homes and all
Her gleaming amethystine wall!

Blind are the guides who know the way,
The guides who write, and preach, and pray,
I watch their lives, and I divine
They differ not from yours and mine!

One man we knew, and only one,
Whose seeking for a city's done,

DEEDS OF MEN

ἄειδε δ' ἄρα κλέα ἀνδρῶν

TO

COLONEL IAN HAMILTON

To you, who know the face of war,
You, that for England wander far,
You that have seen the Ghazis fly
From English lads not sworn to die,
You that have lain where, deadly chill,
The mist crept o'er the Shameful Hill,
You that have conquered, mile by mile,
The currents of unfriendly Nile,
And cheered the march, and eased the strain
When Politics made valour vain,
Ian, to you, from banks of Ken,
We send our lays of Englishmen!

SEEKERS FOR A CITY.

'Believe me, if that blissful, that beautiful place, were set on a hill visible to all the world, I should long ago have journeyed thither. . . . But the number and variety of the ways! For you know, *There is but one road that leads to Corinth.*' HERMOTIMUS (Mr. Pater's Version).

'The Poet says, *dear city of Cecrops*, and wilt thou not say, *dear city of Zeus?*' M. ANTONINUS.

To Corinth leads one road, you say :
  Is there a Corinth, or a way?
Each bland or blatant preacher hath
His painful or his primrose path,
And not a soul of all of these
But knows the city 'twixt the seas,
Her fair unnumbered homes and all
Her gleaming amethystine wall !

Blind are the guides who know the way,
The guides who write, and preach, and pray,
I watch their lives, and I divine
They differ not from yours and mine !

One man we knew, and only one,
Whose seeking for a city 's done,

For what he greatly sought he found,
A city girt with fire around,
A city in an empty land
Between the wastes of sky and sand,
A city on a river-side,
Where by the folk he loved, he died.[1]

Alas! it is not ours to tread
That path wherein his life he led,
Not ours his heart to dare and feel,
Keen as the fragrant Syrian steel;
Yet are we not quite city-less,
Not wholly left in our distress—
Is it not said by One of old,
Sheep have I of another fold?
Ah! faint of heart, and weak of will,
For us there is a city still!

Dear city of Zeus, the Stoic says,[2]
The Voice from Rome's imperial days,
In Thee meet all things, and disperse,
In Thee, for Thee, O Universe!
To me all 's fruit thy seasons bring,
Alike thy summer and thy spring;
The winds that wail, the suns that burn,
From Thee proceed, to Thee return.

January 26, 1885.   [2] M. Antoninus, iv. 23.

Dear city of Zeus, shall *we* not say,
Home to which none can lose the way !
Born in that city's flaming bound,
We do not find her, but are found.
Within her wide and viewless wall
The Universe is girdled all.
All joys and pains, all wealth and dearth,
All things that travail on the earth,
God's will they work, if God there be,
If not, what is my life to me ?

Seek we no further, but abide
Within this city great and wide,
In her and for her living, we
Have no less joy than to be free ;
Nor death nor grief can quite appal
The folk that dwell within her wall,
Nor aught but with our will befall !

THE WHITE PACHA.

VAIN is the dream! However Hope may rave,
    He perished with the folk he could not save,
And though none surely told us he is dead,
And though perchance another in his stead,
Another, not less brave, when all was done,
Had fled unto the southward and the sun,
Had urged a way by force, or won by guile
To streams remotest of the secret Nile,
Had raised an army of the Desert men,
And, waiting for his hour, had turned again
And fallen on that False Prophet, yet we know
GORDON is dead, and these things are not so!
Nay, not for England's cause, nor to restore
Her trampled flag—for he loved Honour more—
Nay, not for Life, Revenge, or Victory,
Would he have fled, whose hour had dawned to die.
He will not come again, whate'er our need,
He will not come, who is happy, being freed
From the deathly flesh and perishable things,
And lies of statesmen and rewards of kings.

Nay, somewhere by the sacred River's shore
He sleeps like those who shall return no more,
No more return for all the prayers of men—
Arthur and Charles—they never come again!
They shall not wake, though fair the vision seem :
Whate'er sick Hope may whisper, vain the dream!

MIDNIGHT, JANUARY 25, 1886.

TO-MORROW is a year since Gordon died !
 A year ago to-night, the Desert still
Crouched on the spring, and panted for its fill
Of lust and blood. Their old art statesmen plied,
And paltered, and evaded, and denied ;
 Guiltless as yet, except for feeble will,
 And craven heart, and calculated skill
In long delays, of their great homicide.

A year ago to-night 'twas not too late.
 The thought comes through our mirth, again, again ;
Methinks I hear the halting foot of Fate
 Approaching and approaching us ; and then
Comes cackle of the House, and the Debate !
 Enough ; he is forgotten amongst men.

ADVANCE, AUSTRALIA.

ON THE OFFER OF HELP FROM THE AUSTRALIANS AFTER THE FALL OF KHARTOUM.

SONS of the giant Ocean isle
   In sport our friendly foes for long,
Well England loves you, and we smile
When you outmatch us many a while,
   So fleet you are, so keen and strong.

You, like that fairy people set
   Of old in their enchanted sea
Far off from men, might well forget
An elder nation's toil and fret,
   Might heed not aught but game and glee.

But what your fathers were you are
   In lands the fathers never knew,
'Neath skies of alien sign and star
You rally to the English war;
   Your hearts are English, kind and true.

And now, when first on England falls
　The shadow of a darkening fate,
You hear the Mother ere she calls,
You leave your ocean-girdled walls,
　And face her foemen in the gate.

COLONEL BURNABY.

> σὺ δ' ἐν στροφάλιγγι κονίης
> κεῖσο μέγας μεγαλωστί, λελασμένος ἱπποσυνάων.

THOU that on every field of earth and sky
    Didst hunt for Death, who seemed to flee and fear,
How great and greatly fallen dost thou lie
    Slain in the Desert by some wandering spear:
'Not here, alas!' may England say, 'not here
    Nor in this quarrel was it meet to die,
    But in that dreadful battle drawing nigh
To thunder through the Afghan passes sheer:

Like Aias by the ships shouldst thou have stood,
    And in some glen have stayed the stream of flight,
    The bulwark of thy people and their shield,
When Indus or when Helmund ran with blood,
    Till back into the Northland and the Night
    The smitten Eagles scattered from the field.'

MELVILLE AND COGHILL.

(THE PLACE OF THE LITTLE HAND.)

DEAD, with their eyes to the foe,
    Dead, with the foe at their feet,
Under the sky laid low
    Truly their slumber is sweet,
Though the wind from the Camp of the Slain Men blow,
    And the rain on the wilderness beat.

Dead, for they chose to die
    When that wild race was run ;
Dead, for they would not fly,
    Deeming their work undone,
Nor cared to look on the face of the sky,
    Nor loved the light of the sun.

Honour we give them and tears,
    And the flag they died to save,
Rent from the rain of the spears,
    Wet from the war and the wave,
Shall waft men's thoughts through the dust of the years,
    Back to their lonely grave !

RHODOCLEIA

TO RHODOCLEIA

ON HER MELANCHOLY SINGING.

(Rhodocleia was beloved by Rufinus, one of the late poets of the Greek Anthology.)

STILL, Rhodocleia, brooding on the dead,
    Still singing of the meads of asphodel,
        Lands desolate of delight?
Say, hast thou dreamed of, or rememberèd,
    The shores where shadows dwell,
        Nor know the sun, nor see the stars of night?

There, 'midst thy music, doth thy spirit gaze
    As a girl pines for home,
    Looking along the way that she hath come,
Sick to return, and counts the weary days!
So wouldst thou flee
    Back to the multitude whose days are done,
Wouldst taste the fruit that lured Persephone,
The sacrament of death; and die, and be
    No more in the wind and sun!

Thou hast not dreamed it, but rememberèd !
    I know thou hast been there,
Hast seen the stately dwellings of the dead
    Rise in the twilight air,
And crossed the shadowy bridge the spirits tread,
    And climbed the golden stair !

Nay, by thy cloudy hair
    And lips that were so fair,
Sad lips now mindful of some ancient smart,
    And melancholy eyes, the haunt of Care,
I know thee who thou art !
    That Rhodocleia, Glory of the Rose,
Of Hellas, ere her close,
    That Rhodocleia who, when all was done
    The golden time of Greece, and fallen her sun,
Swayed her last poet's heart.

With roses did he woo thee, and with song,
    With thine own rose, and with the lily sweet,
        The dark-eyed violet,
        Garlands of wind-flowers wet,
And fragrant love-lamps that the whole night long
        Burned till the dawn was burning in the skies,
        Praising *thy golden eyes,*
And feet more silvery than Thetis' feet!

But thou didst die and flit
    Among the tribes outworn,
        The unavailing myriads of the past :
Oft he beheld thy face in dreams of morn,
And, waking, wept for it,
        Till his own time came at last,
    And then he sought thee in the dusky land !
Wide are the populous places of the dead
Where souls on earth once wed
    May never meet, nor each take other's hand,
Each far from the other fled !

So all in vain he sought for thee, but thou
    Didst never taste of the Lethæan stream,
        Nor that forgetful fruit,
    The mystic pom'granate ;
But from the Mighty Warden fledst ; and now,
    The fugitive of Fate,
    Thou farest in our life as in a dream,
        Still wandering with thy lute,
Like that sweet paynim lady of old song,
Who sang and wandered long,
    For love of her Aucassin, seeking him !
So with thy minstrelsy
    Thou roamest, dreaming of the country dim,
Below the veilèd sky !

There doth thy lover dwell,
    Singing, and seeking still to find thy face
    In that forgetful place :
        Thou shalt not meet him here,
        Not till thy singing clear
Through all the murmur of the streams of hell
        Wins to the Maiden's ear !
May she, perchance, have pity on thee and call
        Thine eager spirit to sit beside her feet,
Passing throughout the long unechoing hall
    Up to the shadowy throne,
        Where the lost lovers of the ages meet ;
    Till then thou art alone !

AVE

' Our Faith and Troth
All time and space controules
Above the highest sphere we meet
Unseen, unknowne, and greet as Angels greet'
        Col. RICHARD LOVELACE. 1649

CLEVEDON CHURCH.

In Memoriam
H. B.

Westward I watch the low green hills of Wales,
   The low sky silver grey,
The turbid Channel with the wandering sails
   Moans through the winter day.
There is no colour but one ashen light
   On tower and lonely tree,
The little church upon the windy height
   Is grey as sky or sea.
But there hath he that woke the sleepless Love
   Slept through these fifty years,
There is the grave that has been wept above
   With more than mortal tears.
And far below I hear the Channel sweep
   And all his waves complain,
As Hallam's dirge through all the years must keep
   Its monotone of pain.

     *   *   *   *   *

Grey sky, brown waters, as a bird that flies,
  My heart flits forth from these
Back to the winter rose of northern skies,
  Back to the northern seas.
And lo, the long waves of the ocean beat
  Below the minster grey,
Caverns and chapels worn of saintly feet,
  And knees of them that pray.
And I remember me how twain were one
  Beside that ocean dim,
I count the years passed over since the sun
  That lights me looked on him,
And dreaming of the voice that, save in sleep,
  Shall greet me not again,
Far, far below I hear the Channel sweep
  And all his waves complain.

TWILIGHT ON TWEED.

THREE crests against the saffron sky,
    Beyond the purple plain,
The kind remembered melody
    Of Tweed once more again.

Wan water from the border hills,
    Dear voice from the old years,
Thy distant music lulls and stills,
    And moves to quiet tears.

Like a loved ghost thy fabled flood
    Fleets through the dusky land;
Where Scott, come home to die, has stood,
    My feet returning stand.

A mist of memory broods and floats,
    The Border waters flow;
The air is full of ballad notes,
    Borne out of long ago.

Old songs that sung themselves to me,
  Sweet through a boy's day dream,
While trout below the blossom'd tree
  Plashed in the golden stream.

   *   *   *   *   *

Twilight, and Tweed, and Eildon Hill,
  Fair and too fair you be ;
You tell me that the voice is still
  That should have welcomed me.

                        1870.

METEMPSYCHOSIS.

I 'SHALL not see thee, nay, but I shall know
   Perchance, the grey eyes in another's eyes,
Shall guess thy curls in gracious locks that flow
   On purest brows, yea, and the swift surmise
   Shall follow and track, and find thee in disguise
Of all sad things, and fair, where sunsets glow,
When through the scent of heather, faint and low,
   The weak wind whispers to the day that dies.

From all sweet art, and out of all old rhyme,
   Thine eyes and lips are light and song to me ;
The shadows of the beauty of all time,
   In song or story are but shapes of thee ;
Alas, the shadowy shapes ! ah, sweet my dear,
   Shall life or death bring all thy being near ?

LOST IN HADES.

I DREAMED that somewhere in the shadowy place,
    Grief of farewell unspoken was forgot
  In welcome, and regret remembered not ;
And hopeless prayer accomplished turned to praise
On lips that had been songless many days ;
    Hope had no more to hope for, and desire
    And dread were overpast, in white attire
New born we walked among the new world's ways.

Then from the press of shades a spirit threw
    Towards me such apples as these gardens bear ;
And turning, I was 'ware of her, and knew
    And followed her fleet voice and flying hair,—
Followed, and found her not, and seeking you
    I found you never, dearest, anywhere.

A STAR IN THE NIGHT.

THE perfect piteous beauty of thy face
    Is like a star the dawning drives away;
Mine eyes may never see in the bright day
Thy pallid halo, thy supernal grace;
But in the night from forth the silent place
    Thou comest, dim in dreams, as doth a stray
    Star of the starry flock that in the grey
Is seen, and lost, and seen a moment's space.

And as the earth at night turns to a star,
    Loved long ago, and dearer than the sun,
So in the spiritual place afar,
    At night our souls are mingled and made one,
And wait till one night fall, and one dawn rise,
That brings no noon too splendid for your eyes.

A SUNSET ON YARROW.

THE wind and the day had lived together,
    They died together, and far away
Spoke farewell in the sultry weather,
Out of the sunset, over the heather,
    The dying wind and the dying day.

Far in the south, the summer levin
    Flushed, a flame in the grey soft air:
We seemed to look on the hills of heaven;
You saw within, but to me 'twas given
    To see your face, as an angel's, there.

Never again, ah surely never
    Shall we wait and watch, where of old we stood,
The low good-night of the hill and the river,
The faint light fade, and the wan stars quiver,
    Twain grown one in the solitude.

ANOTHER WAY.

COME to me in my dreams, and then,
  One saith, I shall be well again,
' For then the night will more than pay
The hopeless longing of the day.

Nay, come not *thou* in dreams, my sweet,
With shadowy robes, and silent feet,
And with the voice, and with the eyes
That greet me in a soft surprise.

Last night, last night, in dreams we met,
And how, to-day, shall I forget,
Or how, remembering, restrain
Mine incommunicable pain?

Nay, where thy land and people are,
Dwell thou remote, apart, afar,
Nor mingle with the shapes that sweep
The melancholy ways of Sleep.

But if, perchance, the shadows break,
If dreams depart, and men awake,
If face to face at length we see,
Be thine the voice to welcome me.

HESPEROTHEN

By the example of certain Grecian mariners, who, being safely returned from the war about Troy, leave yet again their old lands and gods, seeking they know not what, and choosing neither to abide in the fair Phæacian island, nor to dwell and die with the Sirens, at length end miserably in a desert country by the sea, is set forth the *Vanity of Melancholy*. And by the land of Phæacia is to be understood the place of Art and of fair Pleasures; and by Circe's Isle, the place of bodily delights, whereof men, falling aweary, attain to Eld, and to the darkness of that age. Which thing Master Françoys Rabelais feigned, under the similitude of the Isle of the Macræones.

THE SEEKERS FOR PHÆACIA.

THERE is a land in the remotest day,
   Where the soft night is born, and sunset dies;
The eastern shore sees faint tides fade away,
   That wash the lands where laughter, tears, and sighs
Make life,—the lands below the blue of common skies.

But in the west is a mysterious sea,
   (What sails have seen it, or what shipmen known?)
With coasts enchanted where the Sirens be,
   With islands where a Goddess walks alone,
And in the cedar trees the magic winds make moan.

Eastward the human cares of house and home,
   Cities, and ships, and unknown gods, and loves;
Westward, strange maidens fairer than the foam,
   And lawless lives of men, and haunted groves,
Wherein a god may dwell, and where the Dryad roves.

The gods are careless of the days and death
   Of toilsome men, beyond the western seas;

The gods are heedless of their painful breath,
   And love them not, for they are not as these;
But in the golden west they live and lie at ease.

Yet the Phæacians well they love, who live
   At the light's limit, passing careless hours,
Most like the gods; and they have gifts to give,
   Even wine, and fountains musical, and flowers,
And song, and if they will, swift ships, and magic powers.

It is a quiet midland; in the cool
   Of the twilight comes the god, though no man prayed,
To watch the maids and young men beautiful
   Dance, and they see him, and are not afraid,
For they are near of kin to gods, and undismayed.

Ah, would the bright red prows might bring us nigh
   The dreamy isles that the Immortals keep!
But with a mist they hide them wondrously,
   And far the path and dim to where they sleep,—
The loved, the shadowy lands, along the shadowy deep.

A SONG OF PHÆACIA.

THE languid sunset, mother of roses,
    Lingers, a light on the magic seas,
The wide fire flames, as a flower uncloses,
    Heavy with odour, and loose to the breeze.

The red rose clouds, without law or leader,
    Gather and float in the airy plain;
The nightingale sings to the dewy cedar,
    The cedar scatters his scent to the main.

The strange flowers' perfume turns to singing,
    Heard afar over moonlit seas:
The Siren's song, grown faint in winging,
    Falls in scent on the cedar trees.

As waifs blown out of the sunset, flying,
    Purple, and rosy, and grey, the birds
Brighten the air with their wings; their crying
    Wakens a moment the weary herds.

Butterflies flit from the fairy garden,
    Living blossoms of flying flowers;
Never the nights with winter harden,
    Nor moons wax keen in this land of ours.

Great fruits, fragrant, green and golden,
    Gleam in the green, and droop and fall;
Blossom, and bud, and flower unfolden,
    Swing, and cling to the garden wall.

Deep in the woods as twilight darkens,
    Glades are red with the scented fire;
Far in the dells the white maid hearkens,
    Song and sigh of the heart's desire.

Ah, and as moonlight fades in morning,
    Maiden's song in the matin grey,
Faints as the first bird's note, a warning,
    Wakes and wails to the new-born day.

The waking song and the dying measure
    Meet, and the waxing and waning light
Meet, and faint with the hours of pleasure,
    The rose of the sea and the sky is white.

THE DEPARTURE FROM PHÆACIA.

THE PHÆACIANS.

WHY from the dreamy meadows,
    More fair than any dream,
Why seek ye for the shadows
    Beyond the ocean stream?

Through straits of storm and peril,
    Through firths unsailed before,
Why make you for the sterile,
    The dark Kimmerian shore?

There no bright streams are flowing,
    There day and night are one,
No harvest time, no sowing,
    No sight of any sun;

No sound of song or tabor,
    No dance shall greet you there;
No noise of mortal labour
    Breaks on the blind chill air.

Are ours not happy places,
   Where gods with mortals trod?
Saw not our sires the faces
   Of many a present god?

THE SEEKERS.

Nay, now no god comes hither,
   In shape that men may see;
They fare we know not whither,
   We know not what they be.

Yea, though the sunset lingers
   Far in your fairy glades,
Though yours the sweetest singers,
   Though yours the kindest maids,

Yet here be the true shadows,
   Here in the doubtful light;
Amid the dreamy meadows
   No shadow haunts the night.

We seek a city splendid,
   With light beyond the sun;
Or lands where dreams are ended,
   And works and days are done.

A BALLAD OF DEPARTURE.[1]

Fair white bird, what song art thou singing
   In wintry weather of lands o'er sea?
Dear white bird, what way art thou winging,
   Where no grass grows, and no green tree?

I looked at the far-off fields and grey,
   There grew no tree but the cypress tree,
That bears sad fruits with the flowers of May,
   And whoso looks on it, woe is he.

And whoso eats of the fruit thereof
Has no more sorrow, and no more love;
And who sets the same in his garden stead,
In a little space he is waste and dead.

[1] From the Romaic.

THEY HEAR THE SIRENS FOR THE SECOND TIME.

THE weary sails a moment slept,
   The oars were silent for a space,
As past Hesperian shores we swept,
   That were as a remembered face
Seen after lapse of hopeless years,
   In Hades, when the shadows meet,
Dim through the mist of many tears,
   And strange, and though a shadow, sweet.

So seemed the half-remembered shore,
   That slumbered, mirrored in the blue,
With havens where we touched of yore,
   And ports that over well we knew.
Then broke the calm before a breeze
   That sought the secret of the west;
And listless all we swept the seas
   Towards the Islands of the Blest.

Beside a golden sanded bay
   We saw the Sirens, very fair

The flowery hill whereon they lay,
    The flowers set upon their hair.
Their old sweet song came down the wind,
    Remembered music waxing strong,—
Ah now no need of cords to bind,
    No need had we of Orphic song.

It once had seemed a little thing
    To lay our lives down at their feet,
That dying we might hear them sing,
    And dying see their faces sweet;
But now, we glanced, and passing by,
    No care had we to tarry long;
Faint hope, and rest, and memory
    Were more than any Siren's song.

CIRCE'S ISLE REVISITED.

AH, Circe, Circe ! in the wood we cried ;
   Ah, Circe, Circe ! but no voice replied ;
  No voice from bowers o'ergrown and ruinous
As fallen rocks upon the mountain side.

There was no sound of singing in the air ;
Faded or fled the maidens that were fair,
  No more for sorrow or joy were seen of us,
No light of laughing eyes, or floating hair.

The perfume, and the music, and the flame
Had passed away ; the memory of shame
  Alone abode, and stings of faint desire,
And pulses of vague quiet went and came.

Ah, Circe ! in thy sad changed fairy place,
Our dead youth came and looked on us a space,
  With drooping wings, and eyes of faded fire,
And wasted hair about a weary face.

CIRCE'S ISLE REVISITED

Why had we ever sought the magic isle
That seemed so happy in the days erewhile?
  Why did we ever leave it, where we met
A world of happy wonders in one smile?

Back to the westward and the waning light
We turned, we fled; the solitude of night
  Was better than the infinite regret,
In fallen places of our dead delight.

THE LIMIT OF LANDS.

BETWEEN the circling ocean sea
    And the poplars of Persephone
There lies a strip of barren sand,
Flecked with the sea's last spray, and strown
With waste leaves of the poplars, blown
    From gardens of the shadow land.

With altars of old sacrifice
The shore is set, in mournful wise
    The mists upon the ocean brood ;
Between the water and the air
    The clouds are born that float and fare
Between the water and the wood.

Upon the grey sea never sail
Of mortals passed within our hail,
    Where the last weak waves faint and flow ;
We heard within the poplar pale
The murmur of a doubtful wail
    Of voices loved so long ago.

We scarce had care to die or live,
We had no honey cake to give,
   No wine of sacrifice to shed ;
There lies no new path over sea,
And now we know how faint they be,
   The feasts and voices of the dead.

Ah, flowers and dance ! ah, sun and snow !
Glad life, sad life we did forego
   To dream of quietness and rest ;
Ah, would the fleet sweet roses here
Poured light and perfume through the drear
   Pale year, and wan land of the west.

Sad youth, that let the spring go by
Because the spring is swift to fly,
   Sad youth, that feared to mourn or love,
Behold how sadder far is this,
To know that rest is nowise bliss,
   And darkness is the end thereof.

VERSES

MARTIAL IN TOWN.

'LAST night, within the stifling train,
   Lit by the foggy lamp o'erhead,
  Sick of the sad Last News, I read
Verse of that joyous child of Spain,

Who dwelt when Rome was waxing cold,
  Within the Roman din and smoke.
  And like my heart to me they spoke,
These accents of his heart of old :—

  Brother, had we but time to live,
    And fleet the careless hours together,
  With all that leisure has to give
    Of perfect life and peaceful weather,

  The Rich Man's halls, the anxious faces,
  The weary Forum, courts, and cases
    Should know us not ; but quiet nooks,
  But summer shade by field and well,
    But country rides, and talk of books,
  At home, with these, we fain would dwell!

Now neither lives, but day by day
  Sees the suns wasting in the west,
And feels their flight, and doth delay
  To lead the life he loveth best.

So from thy city prison broke,
  Martial, thy wail for life misspent,
And so, through London's noise and smoke
  My heart replies to the lament.

For dear as Tagus with his gold,
  And swifter Salo, were to thee,
So dear to me the woods that fold
  The streams that circle Fernielea !

APRIL ON TWEED.

AS birds are fain to build their nest
    The first soft sunny day,
So longing wakens in my breast
    A month before the May,
When now the wind is from the West,
    And Winter melts away.

The snow lies yet on Eildon Hill,
    But soft the breezes blow.
If melting snows the waters fill,
    We nothing heed the snow,
But we must up and take our will,—
    A fishing will we go!

Below the branches brown and bare,
    Beneath the primrose lea,
The trout lies waiting for his fare,
    A hungry trout is he;
He's hooked, and springs and splashes there
    Like salmon from the sea!

APRIL ON TWEED

Oh, April tide 's a pleasant tide,
   However times may fall,
And sweet to welcome Spring, the Bride,
   You hear the mavis call ;
But all adown the water-side
   The Spring 's most fair of all.

TIRED OF TOWNS.

'When we spoke to her of the New Jerusalem, she said she would rather go to a country place in Heaven.'   *Letters from the Black Country.*

I'M weary of towns, it seems a'most a pity
   We didn't stop down i' the country and clem,
And you say that I'm bound for another city,
   For the streets o' the New Jerusalem.

And the streets are never like Sheffield, here,
   Nor the smoke don't cling like a smut to *them*;
But the water o' life flows cool and clear
   Through the streets o' the New Jerusalem.

And the houses, you say, are of jasper cut,
   And the gates are gaudy wi' gold and gem;
But there's times I could wish as the gates was shut—
   The gates o' the New Jerusalem.

For I come from a country that's over-built
   Wi' streets that stifle, and walls that hem,
And the gorse on a common's worth all the gilt
   And the gold of your New Jerusalem.

And I hope that they'll bring me, in Paradise,
    To green lanes leafy wi' bough and stem—
To a country place in the land o' the skies,
    And not to the New Jerusalem.

SCYTHE SONG.

MOWERS, weary and brown, and blithe,
  What is the word methinks ye know,
Endless over-word that the Scythe
  Sings to the blades of the grass below?
Scythes that swing in the grass and clover,
  Something, still, they say as they pass;
What is the word that, over and over,
  Sings the Scythe to the flowers and grass?

Hush, ah hush, the Scythes are saying,
  Hush, and heed not, and fall asleep;
Hush, they say to the grasses swaying,
  Hush, they sing to the clover deep!
Hush—'tis the lullaby Time is singing—
  Hush, and heed not, for all things pass,
Hush, ah hush! and the Scythes are swinging
  Over the clover, over the grass!

PEN AND INK.

YE wanderers that were my sires,
    Who read men's fortunes in the hand,
Who voyaged with your smithy fires
    From waste to waste across the land,
Why did you leave for garth and town
    Your life by heath and river's brink,
Why lay your gipsy freedom down
    And doom your child to Pen and Ink?

You wearied of the wild-wood meal
    That crowned, or failed to crown, the day;
Too honest or too tame to steal
    You broke into the beaten way:
Plied loom or awl like other men,
    And learned to love the guineas' chink—
Oh, recreant sires, who doomed me then
    To earn so few—with Pen and Ink!

Where it hath fallen the tree must lie.
    'Tis over late for *me* to roam,
Yet the caged bird who hears the cry
    Of his wild fellows fleeting home,

May feel no sharper pang than mine,
   Who seem to hear, whene'er I think,
Spate in the stream, and wind in pine,
   Call me to quit dull Pen and Ink.

For then the spirit wandering,
   That slept within the blood, awakes;
For then the summer and the spring
   I fain would meet by streams and lakes;
But ah, my Birthright long is sold,
   But custom chains me, link on link,
And I must get me, as of old,
   Back to my tools, to Pen and Ink.

A DREAM.

WHY will you haunt my sleep?
   You know it may not be,
The grave is wide and deep,
   That sunders you and me;
In bitter dreams we reap
   The sorrow we have sown,
And I would I were asleep,
   Forgotten and alone!

We knew and did not know,
   We saw and did not see,
The nets that long ago
   Fate wove for you and me;
The cruel nets that keep
   The birds that sob and moan,
And I would we were asleep,
   Forgotten and alone!

*   *   *   *

THE SINGING ROSE.

'*La Rose qui chante et l'herbe qui égare.*'

WHITE Rose on the grey garden wall,
  Where now no night-wind whispereth,
Call to the far-off flowers, and call
  With murmured breath and musical
Till all the Roses hear, and all
  Sing to my Love what the White Rose saith.

White Rose on the grey garden wall
  That long ago we sung!
Again you come at Summer's call,—
Again beneath my windows all
  With trellised flowers is hung,
With clusters of the roses white
Like fragrant stars in a green night.

Once more I hear the sister towers
  Each unto each reply,
The bloom is on those limes of ours,

The weak wind shakes the bloom in showers,
   Snow from a cloudless sky ;
There is no change this happy day
Within the College Gardens grey !

St. Mary's, Merton, Magdalen—still
   Their sweet bells chime and swing,
The old years answer them, and thrill
A wintry heart against its will
   With memories of the Spring—
That Spring we sought the gardens through
For flowers which ne'er in gardens grew !

For we, beside our nurse's knee,
   In fairy tales had heard
Of that strange Rose which blossoms free
On boughs of an enchanted tree,
   And sings like any bird !
And of the weed beside the way
That leadeth lovers' steps astray !

In vain we sought the Singing Rose
   Whereof old legends tell,
Alas, we found it not mid those
Within the grey old College close,
   That budded, flowered, and fell,—
We found that herb called ' Wandering '
And meet no more, no more in Spring !

Yes, unawares the unhappy grass
  That leadeth steps astray,
We trod, and so it came to pass
That never more we twain, alas,
  Shall walk the self-same way.
And each must deem, though neither knows,
' That *neither* found the Singing Rose !

A REVIEW IN RHYME.

A LITTLE of Horace, a little of Prior,
A sketch of a Milkmaid, a lay of the Squire—
These, these are 'on draught' 'At the Sign of the Lyre!'

A child in Blue Ribbons that sings to herself,
A talk of the Books on the Sheraton shelf,
A sword of the Stuarts, a wig of the Guelph,

A *lai*, a *pantoum*, a *ballade*, a *rondeau*,
A pastel by Greuze, and a sketch by Moreau,
And the chimes of the rhymes that sing sweet as they go,

A fan, and a folio, a ringlet, a glove,
'Neath a dance by Laguerre on the ceiling above,
And a dream of the days when the bard was in love,

A scent of dead roses, a glance at a pun,
A toss of old powder, a glint of the sun,
They meet in the volume that Dobson has done!

If there 's more that the heart of a man can desire,
He may search, in his Swinburne, for fury and fire;
If he 's wise—he'll alight 'At the Sign of the Lyre!'

COLINETTE.

FOR A SKETCH BY MR. G. LESLIE, R.A.

FRANCE your country, as we know;
    Room enough for guessing yet,
What lips now or long ago,
    Kissed and named you—Colinette.
In what fields from sea to sea,
    By what stream your home was set,
Loire or Seine was glad of thee,
    Marne or Rhone, O Colinette?

Did you stand with maidens ten,
    Fairer maids were never seen,
When the young king and his men
    Passed among the orchards green?
Nay, old ballads have a note
    Mournful, we would fain forget;
No such sad old air should float
    Round your young brows, Colinette.

Say, did Ronsard sing to you,
    Shepherdess, to lull his pain,
When the court went wandering through
    Rose pleasances of Touraine?
Ronsard and his famous Rose
    Long are dust the breezes fret;
You, within the garden close,
    You are blooming, Colinette.

Have I seen you proud and gay,
    With a patched and perfumed beau,
Dancing through the summer day,
    Misty summer of Watteau?
Nay, so sweet a maid as you
    Never walked a minuet
With the splendid courtly crew;
    Nay, forgive me, Colinette.

Not from Greuze's canvases
    Do you cast a glance, a smile;
You are not as one of these,
    Yours is beauty without guile.
Round your maiden brows and hair
    Maidenhood and Childhood met
Crown and kiss you, sweet and fair,
    New art's blossom, Colinette.

A SUNSET OF WATTEAU.

LUI.

THE silk sail fills, the soft winds wake,
   Arise and tempt the seas;
Our ocean is the Palace lake,
Our waves the ripples that we make
   Among the mirrored trees.

ELLE.

Nay, sweet the shore, and sweet the song,
   And dear the languid dream;
The music mingled all day long
With paces of the dancing throng,
   And murmur of the stream.

An hour ago, an hour ago,
   We rested in the shade;
And now, why should we seek to know
What way the wilful waters flow?
   There is no fairer glade.

LUI.

Nay, pleasure flits, and we must sail,
    And seek him everywhere ;
Perchance in sunset's golden pale
He listens to the nightingale,
    Amid the perfumed air.

Come, he has fled ; you are not you,
    And I no more am I ;
Delight is changeful as the hue
Of heaven, that is no longer blue
    In yonder sunset sky.

ELLE.

Nay, if we seek we shall not find,
    If we knock none openeth ;
Nay, see, the sunset fades behind
The mountains, and the cold night wind
    Blows from the house of Death.

NIGHTINGALE WEATHER.

> 'Serai-je nonnette, oui ou non ?
> Serai-je nonnette ? je crois que non.
> Derrière chez mon père
> Il est un bois taillis,
> Le rossignol y chante
> Et le jour et la nuit.
> Il chante pour les filles
> Qui n'ont pas d'ami ;
> Il ne chant pas pour moi,
> J'en ai un, Dieu merci.'—*Old French.*

I'LL never be a nun, I trow,
   While apple bloom is white as snow,
  But far more fair to see ;
I'll never wear nun's black and white
While nightingales make sweet the night
   Within the apple tree.

Ah, listen ! 'tis the nightingale,
And in the wood he makes his wail,
   Within the apple tree ;
He singeth of the sore distress
Of many ladies loverless ;
   Thank God, no song for me.

For when the broad May moon is low,
A gold fruit seen where blossoms blow
   In the boughs of the apple tree,
A step I know is at the gate ;
Ah love, but it is long to wait
   Until night's noon bring thee !

Between lark's song and nightingale's
A silent space, while dawning pales,
   The birds leave still and free
For words and kisses musical,
For silence and for sighs that fall
   In the dawn, 'twixt him and me.

LOVE AND WISDOM.

> 'When last we gathered roses in the garden
> I found my wits, but truly you lost yours.'
> *The Broken Heart.*

JULY and June brought flowers and love
   To you, but I would none thereof,
Whose heart kept all through summer time
A flower of frost and winter rime.
Yours was true wisdom—was it not?
Even love; but I had clean forgot,
Till seasons of the falling leaf,
All loves, but one that turned to grief.
At length at touch of autumn tide
When roses fell, and summer died,
All in a dawning deep with dew,
Love flew to me, Love fled from you.
The roses drooped their weary heads,
I spoke among the garden beds;
You would not hear, you could not know,
Summer and love seemed long ago,
As far, as faint, as dim a dream,
As to the dead this world may seem.

Ah sweet, in winter's miseries,
Perchance you may remember this,
How Wisdom was not justified
In summer time or autumn tide,
Though for this once below the sun,
Wisdom and Love were made at one ;
But Love was bitter-bought enough,
And Wisdom light of wing as Love.

GOOD-BYE.

KISS me, and say good-bye;
    Good-bye, there is no word to say but this,
  Nor any lips left for my lips to kiss,
Nor any tears to shed, when these tears dry;
Kiss me, and say, good-bye.

Farewell, be glad, forget;
    There is no need to say 'forget,' I know,
    For youth is youth, and time will have it so,
And though your lips are pale, and your eyes wet,
    Farewell, you must forget.

You shall bring home your sheaves,
    Many, and heavy, and with blossoms twined
    Of memories that go not out of mind;
Let this one sheaf be twined with poppy leaves
When you bring home your sheaves.

In garnered loves of thine,
    The ripe good fruit of many hearts and years,
    Somewhere let this lie, grey and salt with tears;
It grew too near the sea wind, and the brine
Of life, this love of mine.

This sheaf was spoiled in spring,
    And over-long was green, and early sere,
    And never gathered gold in the late year
From autumn suns, and moons of harvesting,
But failed in frosts of spring.

Yet was it thine, my sweet,
    This love, though weak as young corn withered,
    Whereof no man may gather and make bread;
Thine, though it never knew the summer heat;
Forget not quite, my sweet.

AN OLD PRAYER.

Χαῖρέ μοι, ὦ βασίλεια, διαμπερὲς, εἰς ὅ κε γῆρας
Ἔλθῃ καὶ θάνατος, τά τ' ἐπ' ἀνθρώποισι πέλονται.
Odyssey, XIII.

MY prayer an old prayer borroweth,
    Of ancient love and memory—
' Do thou farewell, till Eld and Death,
That come to all men, come to thee.'
Gently as winter's early breath,
Scarce felt, what time the swallows flee,
To lands whereof no man knoweth
Of summer, over land and sea;
So with thy soul may summer be,
Even as the ancient singer saith,
' Do thou farewell, till Eld and Death,
That come to all men, come to thee.'

À LA BELLE HÉLÈNE.

AFTER RONSARD.

More closely than the clinging vine
   About the wedded tree,
Clasp thou thine arms, ah, mistress mine !
   About the heart of me.
Or seem to sleep, and stoop your face
   Soft on my sleeping eyes,
Breathe in your life, your heart, your grace,
   Through me, in kissing wise.
Bow down, bow down your face, I pray,
   To me, that swoon to death,
Breathe back the life you kissed away,
   Breathe back your kissing breath.
So by your eyes I swear and say,
   My mighty oath and sure,
From your kind arms no maiden may
   My loving heart allure.
I'll bear your yoke, that's light enough,
   And to the Elysian plain,

When we are dead of love, my love,
    One boat shall bear us twain.
They'll flock around you, fleet and fair,
    All true loves that have been,
And you of all the shadows there,
    Shall be the shadow queen.
Ah, shadow-loves and shadow-lips !
    Ah, while 'tis called to-day,
Love me, my love, for summer slips,
    And August ebbs away.

SYLVIE ET AURÉLIE.

IN MEMORY OF GÉRARD DE NERVAL.

TWO loves there were, and one was born
    Between the sunset and the rain;
Her singing voice went through the corn,
Her dance was woven 'neath the thorn,
    On grass the fallen blossoms stain;
And suns may set, and moons may wane,
But this love comes no more again.

There were two loves and one made white,
    Thy singing lips, and golden hair;
Born of the city's mire and light,
The shame and splendour of the night,
    She trapped and fled thee unaware;
Not through the lamplight and the rain
Shalt thou behold this love again.

Go forth and seek, by wood and hill,
    Thine ancient love of dawn and dew;
There comes no voice from mere or rill,

Her dance is over, fallen still
   The ballad burdens that she knew:
And thou must wait for her in vain,
Till years bring back thy youth again.

That other love, afield, afar
   Fled the light love, with lighter feet.
Nay, though thou seek where gravesteads are,
And flit in dreams from star to star,
   That dead love shalt thou never meet,
Till through bleak dawn and blowing rain
Thy soul shall find her soul again.

A LOST PATH.

Plotinus, the Greek philosopher, had a certain proper mode of ecstasy, whereby, as Porphyry saith, his soul, becoming free from his deathly flesh, was made one with the Spirit that is in the world.

ALAS, the path is lost, we cannot leave
   Our bright, our clouded life, and pass away
As through strewn clouds, that stain the quiet eve,
   To heights remoter of the purer day.
The soul may not, returning whence she came,
   Bathe herself deep in Being, and forget
The joys that fever, and the cares that fret,
   Made once more one with the eternal flame
   That breathes in all things ever more the same.
She would be young again, thus drinking deep
   Of her old life; and this has been, men say,
But this we know not, who have only sleep
   To soothe us, sleep more terrible than day,
Where dead delights, and fair lost faces stray,
   To make us weary at our wakening;
And of that long lost path to the Divine
We dream, as some Greek shepherd erst might sing,
   Half credulous, of easy Proserpine,
And of the lands that lie 'beneath the day's decline.'

THE SHADE OF HELEN.

Some say that Helen went never to Troy, but abode in Egypt; for the gods, having made in her semblance a woman out of clouds and shadows, sent the same to be wife to Paris. For this shadow then the Greeks and Trojans slew each other.

WHY from the quiet hollows of the hills,
    And extreme meeting place of light and shade,
Wherein soft rains fell slowly, and became
Clouds among sister clouds, where fair spent beams
And dying glories of the sun would dwell,
Why have they whom I know not, nor may know,
Strange hands, unseen and ruthless, fashioned me,
And borne me from the silent shadowy hills,
Hither, to noise and glow of alien life,
To harsh and clamorous swords, and sound of war?

One speaks unto me words that would be sweet,
Made harsh, made keen with love that knows me not.
And some strange force, within me or around,
Makes answer, kiss for kiss, and sigh for sigh,
And somewhere there is fever in the halls
That troubles me, for no such trouble came
To vex the cool far hollows of the hills.

The foolish folk crowd round me, and they cry,
That house, and wife, and lands, and all Troy town,
Are little to lose, if they may keep me here,
And see me flit, a pale and silent shade,
Among the streets bereft, and helpless shrines.

At other hours another life seems mine,
Where one great river runs unswollen of rain,
By pyramids of unremembered kings,
And homes of men obedient to the Dead.
There dark and quiet faces come and go
Around me, then again the shriek of arms,
And all the turmoil of the Ilian men.

What are they? even shadows such as I.
What make they? Even this—the sport of gods—
The sport of gods, however free they seem.
Ah, would the game were ended, and the light,
The blinding light, and all too mighty suns,
Withdrawn, and I once more with sister shades,
Unloved, forgotten, mingled with the mist,
Dwelt in the hollows of the shadowy hills.

SONNETS

SHE.

TO H. R. H.

NOT in the waste beyond the swamps and sand,
    The fever-haunted forest and lagoon,
Mysterious Kôr thy walls forsaken stand,
    Thy lonely towers beneath the lonely moon,
    Not there doth Ayesha linger, rune by rune
Spelling strange scriptures of a people banned.
    The world is disenchanted; over soon
Shall Europe send her spies through all the land.

Nay, not in Kôr, but in whatever spot,
    In town or field, or by the insatiate sea,
Men brood on buried loves, and unforgot,
    Or break themselves on some divine decree,
Or would o'erleap the limits of their lot,
    There, in the tombs and deathless, dwelleth SHE!

HERODOTUS IN EGYPT.

HE left the land of youth, he left the young,
    The smiling gods of Greece ; he passed the isle
Where Jason loitered, and where Sappho sung,
    He sought the secret-founted wave of Nile,
    And of their old world, dead a weary while,
Heard the priests murmur in their mystic tongue,
    And through the fanes went voyaging, among
Dark tribes that worshipped Cat and Crocodile.

He learned the tales of death Divine and birth,
Strange loves of Hawk and Serpent, Sky and Earth,
    The marriage, and the slaying of the Sun.
The shrines of gods and beasts he wandered through,
And mocked not at their godhead, for he knew
    Behind all creeds the Spirit that is One.

GÉRARD DE NERVAL.

OF all that were thy prisons—ah, untamed,
    Ah, light and sacred soul!—none holds thee now;
  No wall, no bar, no body of flesh, but thou
Art free and happy in the lands unnamed,
Within whose gates, on weary wings and maimed,
    Thou still would'st bear that mystic golden bough
    The Sibyl doth to singing men allow,
Yet thy report folk heeded not, but blamed.
    And they would smile and wonder, seeing where
Thou stood'st, to watch light leaves, or clouds, or wind,
    Dreamily murmuring a ballad air,
Caught from the Valois peasants; dost thou find
    A new life gladder than the old times were,
A love more fair than Sylvie, and as kind?

RONSARD.

MASTER, I see thee with the locks of grey,
    Crowned by the Muses with the laurel-wreath;
I see the roses hiding underneath,
Cassandra's gift; she was less dear than they.
Thou, Master, first hast roused the lyric lay,
    The sleeping song that the dead years bequeath,
    Hast sung thine answer to the lays that breathe
Through ages, and through ages far away.

And thou hast heard the pulse of Pindar beat,
    Known Horace by the fount Bandusian!
Their deathless line thy living strains repeat,
    But ah, thy voice is sad, thy roses wan,
But ah, thy honey is not honey-sweet,
    Thy bees have fed on yews Sardinian!

LOVE'S MIRACLE.

WITH other helpless folk about the gate,
    The gate called Beautiful, with weary eyes
That take no pleasure in the summer skies,
Nor all things that are fairest, does she wait;
So bleak a time, so sad a changeless fate
    Makes her with dull experience early wise,
    And in the dawning and the sunset, sighs
That all hath been, and shall be, desolate.

Ah, if Love come not soon, and bid her live,
    And know herself the fairest of fair things,
Ah, if he have no healing gift to give,
    Warm from his breast, and holy from his wings,
Or if at least Love's shadow in passing by
Touch not and heal her, surely she must die.

DREAMS.

HE spake not truth, however wise, who said
    That happy, and that hapless men in sleep
Have equal fortune, fallen from care as deep
As countless, careless, races of the dead.
Not so, for alien paths of dreams we tread,
    And one beholds the faces that he sighs
    In vain to bring before his daylit eyes,
And waking, he remembers on his bed ;

And one with fainting heart and feeble hand
Fights a dim battle in a doubtful land
    Where strength and courage were of no avail ;
And one is borne on fairy breezes far
To the bright harbours of a golden star
    Down fragrant fleeting waters rosy pale.

TWO SONNETS OF THE SIRENS.

' Les Sirènes estoient tant intimes amies et fidelles compagnes de Proserpine, qu'elles estoient toujours ensemble. Esmues du juste deuil de la perte de leur chère compagne, et enuyées jusques au desespoir, elles s'arrestèrent à la mer Sicilienne, où par leurs chants elles attiroient les navigans, mais l'unique fin de la volupté de leur musique est la Mort.'   PONTUS DE TYARD, 1570.

THE Sirens once were maidens innocent
    That through the water-meads with Proserpine
Plucked no fire-hearted flowers, but were content
    Cool fritillaries and flag-flowers to twine,
    With lilies woven and with wet woodbine ;
Till once they sought the bright Ætnæan flowers,
And their glad mistress fled from summer hours
    With Hades, far from olive, corn, and vine.
And they have sought her all the wide world through
    Till many years, and wisdom, and much wrong
Have filled and changed their song, and o'er the blue
    Rings deadly sweet the magic of the song,
And whoso hears must listen till he die
Far on the flowery shores of Sicily.

So is it with this singing art of ours,
    That once with maids went maidenlike, and played
    With woven dances in the poplar-shade,
And all her song was but of lady's bowers
And the returning swallows, and spring flowers,
    Till forth to seek a shadow-queen she strayed,
    A shadowy land ; and now hath overweighed
Her singing chaplet with the snow and showers.
Yes, fair well-water for the bitter brine
    She left, and by the margin of life's sea
        Sings, and her song is full of the sea's moan,
And wild with dread, and love of Proserpine ;
    And whoso once has listened to her, he
        His whole life long is slave to her alone.

TRANSLATIONS

HYMN TO THE WINDS.

THE WINDS ARE INVOKED BY THE WINNOWERS OF CORN.

DU BELLAY, 1550.

TO you, troop so fleet,
    That with winged wandering feet,
  Through the wide world pass,
And with soft murmuring
Toss the green shades of spring
  In woods and grass,
Lily and violet
I give, and blossoms wet,
  Roses and dew ;
This branch of blushing roses,
Whose fresh bud uncloses,
  Wind-flowers too.

Ah, winnow with sweet breath,
Winnow the holt and heath,
  Round this retreat ;
Where all the golden morn
We fan the gold o' the corn,
  In the sun's heat.

MOONLIGHT.

JACQUES TAHUREAU.

THE high Midnight was garlanding her head
   With many a shining star in shining skies,
And, of her grace, a slumber on mine eyes,
   And, after sorrow, quietness was shed.
Far in dim fields cicalas jargonèd
   A thin shrill clamour of complaints and cries;
And all the woods were pallid, in strange wise,
   With pallor of the sad moon overspread.

Then came my lady to that lonely place,
And, from her palfrey stooping, did embrace
   And hang upon my neck, and kissed me over;
Wherefore the day is far less dear than night,
And sweeter is the shadow than the light,
   Since night has made me such a happy lover.

THE GRAVE AND THE ROSE.

VICTOR HUGO.

THE Grave said to the Rose,
   'What of the dews of morn,
Love's flower, what end is theirs?'
   'And what of souls outworn,
Of them whereon doth close
   The tomb's mouth unawares?'
The Rose said to the Grave.

The Rose said, 'In the shade
   From the dawn's tears is made
A perfume faint and strange,
   Amber and honey sweet.'
   'And all the spirits fleet
Do suffer a sky-change,
   More strangely than the dew,
   To God's own angels new,'
The Grave said to the Rose.

A VOW TO HEAVENLY VENUS.

DU BELLAY.

WE that with like hearts love, we lovers twain,
    New wedded in the village by thy fane,
Lady of all chaste love, to thee it is
We bring these amaranths, these white lilies,
A sign, and sacrifice; may Love, we pray,
Like amaranthine flowers, feel no decay;
Like these cool lilies may our loves remain,
Perfect and pure, and know not any stain;
And be our hearts, from this thy holy hour,
Bound each to each, like flower to wedded flower.

OF HIS LADY'S OLD AGE.

RONSARD.

WHEN you are very old, at evening
    You'll sit and spin beside the fire, and say,
Humming my songs, 'Ah well, ah well-a-day!
When I was young, of me did Ronsard sing.'
None of your maidens that doth hear the thing,
    Albeit with her weary task foredone,
    But wakens at my name, and calls you one
Blest, to be held in long remembering.

I shall be low beneath the earth, and laid
On sleep, a phantom in the myrtle shade,
    While you beside the fire, a grandame grey,
My love, your pride, remember and regret;
Ah, love me, love! we may be happy yet,
    And gather roses, while 't is called to-day.

SHADOWS OF HIS LADY.

JACQUES TAHUREAU.

WITHIN the sand of what far river lies
    The gold that gleams in tresses of my Love?
What highest circle of the Heavens above
Is jewelled with such stars as are her eyes?
And where is the rich sea whose coral vies
    With her red lips, that cannot kiss enough?
What dawn-lit garden knew the rose, whereof
    The fled soul lives in her cheeks' rosy guise?

What Parian marble that is loveliest
Can match the whiteness of her brow and breast?
    When drew she breath from the Sabæan glade?
Oh happy rock and river, sky and sea,
Gardens, and glades Sabæan, all that be
    The far-off splendid semblance of my maid!

APRIL.

RÉMY BELLEAU, 1560.

APRIL, pride of woodland ways,
    Of glad days,
April, bringing hope of prime,
    To the young flowers that beneath
    Their bud sheath
Are guarded in their tender time;

April, pride of fields that be
    Green and free,
That in fashion glad and gay,
Stud with flowers red and blue,
    Every hue,
Their jewelled spring array;

April, pride of murmuring
    Winds of spring,
That beneath the winnowed air,
Trap with subtle nets and sweet
    Flora's feet,
Flora's feet, the fleet and fair;

April, by thy hand caressed,
    From her breast,
Nature scatters everywhere
Handfuls of all sweet perfumes,
    Buds and blooms,
Making faint the earth and air.

April, joy of the green hours,
    Clothes with flowers
Over all her locks of gold
My sweet Lady; and her breast
    With the blest
Buds of summer manifold.

April, with thy gracious wiles,
    Like the smiles,
Smiles of Venus; and thy breath
Like her breath, the gods' delight,
    (From their height
They take the happy air beneath;)

It is thou that, of thy grace,
    From their place
In the far-off isles dost bring
Swallows over earth and sea,
    Glad to be
Messengers of thee, and Spring.

Daffodil and eglantine,
    And woodbine,
Lily, violet, and rose
Plentiful in April fair,
    To the air,
Their pretty petals to unclose.

Nightingales ye now may hear,
    Piercing clear,
Singing in the deepest shade ;
Many and many a babbled note
    Chime and float,
Woodland music through the glade.

April, all to welcome thee,
    Spring sets free
Ancient flames, and with low breath
Wakes the ashes grey and old
    That the cold
Chilled within our hearts to death.

Thou beholdest in the warm
    Hours, the swarm
Of the thievish bees, that flies
Evermore from bloom to bloom
    For perfume,
Hid away in tiny thighs.

Her cool shadows May can boast,
    Fruits almost
Ripe, and gifts of fertile dew,
Manna-sweet and honey-sweet,
    That complete
Her flower garland fresh and new.

Nay, but I will give my praise
    To these days,
    Named with the glad name of Her [1]
That from out the foam o' the sea
    Came to be
Sudden light on earth and air.

[1] Aphrodite—Avril.

AN OLD TUNE.

GÉRARD DE NERVAL.

THERE is an air for which I would disown
    Mozart's, Rossini's, Weber's melodies,—
A sweet sad air that languishes and sighs,
    And keeps its secret charm for me alone.

Whene'er I hear that music vague and old,
    Two hundred years are mist that rolls away;
The thirteenth Louis reigns, and I behold
    A green land golden in the dying day.

An old red castle, strong with stony towers,
    The windows gay with many-coloured glass;
Wide plains, and rivers flowing among flowers,
    That bathe the castle basement as they pass.

In antique weed, with dark eyes and gold hair,
    A lady looks forth from her window high;
It may be that I knew and found her fair,
    In some forgotten life, long time gone by.

OLD LOVES.

HENRI MURGER.

LOUISE, have you forgotten yet
    The corner of the flowery land,
The ancient garden where we met,
    My hand that trembled in your hand?
Our lips found words scarce sweet enough,
    As low beneath the willow-trees
We sat; have you forgotten, love?
    Do you remember, love Louise?

Marie, have you forgotten yet
    The loving barter that we made?
The rings we changed, the suns that set,
    The woods fulfilled with sun and shade?
The fountains that were musical
    By many an ancient trysting tree—
Marie, have you forgotten all?
    Do you remember, love Marie?

Christine, do you remember yet
    Your room with scents and roses gay?
My garret—near the sky 'twas set—
    The April hours, the nights of May?
The clear calm nights—the stars above
    That whispered they were fairest seen
Through no cloud-veil? Remember, love!
    Do you remember, love Christine?

Louise is dead, and, well-a-day!
    Marie a sadder path has ta'en;
And pale Christine has passed away
    In southern suns to bloom again.
Alas! for one and all of us—
    Marie, Louise, Christine forget;
Our bower of love is ruinous,
    And I alone remember yet.

A LADY OF HIGH DEGREE.

*I be pareld most of prise,
I ride after the wild fee.*

WILL ye that I should sing
　　Of the love of a goodly thing,
Was no vilein's may?
'Tis all of a knight so free,
Under the olive tree,
　Singing this lay.

Her weed was of samite fine,
Her mantle of white ermine,
　Green silk her hose;
Her shoon with silver gay,
Her sandals flowers of May,
　Laced small and close.

Her belt was of fresh spring buds,
Set with gold clasps and studs,
　Fine linen her shift;
Her purse it was of love,
Her chain was the flower thereof,
　And Love's gift.

Upon a mule she rode,
The selle was of brent gold,
   The bits of silver made;
Three red rose trees there were
That overshadowed her,
   For a sun shade.

She riding on a day,
Knights met her by the way,
   They did her grace:
'Fair lady, whence be ye?'
'France it is my countrie,
   I come of a high race.

'My sire is the nightingale,
That sings, making his wail,
   In the wild wood, clear;
The mermaid is mother to me,
That sings in the salt sea,
   In the ocean mere.'

'Ye come of a right good race,
And are born of a high place,
   And of high degree;
Would to God that ye were
Given unto me, being fair,
   My lady and love to be.'

IANNOULA.

ROMAIC FOLK-SONG.

ALL the maidens were merry and wed
    All to lovers so fair to see ;
The lover I took to my bridal bed
    He is not long for love and me.

I spoke to him and he nothing said,
    I gave him bread of the wheat so fine ;
He did not eat of the bridal bread,
    He did not drink of the bridal wine.

I made him a bed was soft and deep,
    I made him a bed to sleep with me ;
' Look on me once before you sleep,
    And look on the flower of my fair body.

' Flowers of April, and fresh May-dew,
    Dew of April and buds of May ;
Two white blossoms that bud for you,
    Buds that blossom before the day.'

THE MILK-WHITE DOE.

FRENCH VOLKS-LIED.

IT was a mother and a maid
   That walked the woods among,
And still the maid went slow and sad,
   And still the mother sung.

'What ails you, daughter Margaret?
   Why go you pale and wan?
Is it for a cast of bitter love,
   Or for a false leman?'

'It is not for a false lover
   That I go sad to see;
But it is for a weary life
   Beneath the greenwood tree.

'For ever in the good daylight
   A maiden may I go,
But always on the ninth midnight
   I change to a milk-white doe.

'They hunt me through the green forest
  With hounds and hunting men;
And ever it is my fair brother
  That is so fierce and keen.'

* * * * *

'Good-morrow, mother.' 'Good-morrow, son;
  Where are your hounds so good?'
'Oh, they are hunting a white doe
  Within the glad greenwood.

'And three times have they hunted her,
  And thrice she's won away;
The fourth time that they follow her
  That white doe they shall slay.'

* * * * *

Then out and spoke the forester,
  As he came from the wood,
'Now never saw I maid's gold hair
  Among the wild deer's blood.

'And I have hunted the wild deer
  In east lands and in west;
And never saw I white doe yet
  That had a maiden's breast.'

Then up and spake her fair brother,
    Between the wine and bread :
' Behold I had but one sister,
    And I have been her dead.

' But ye must bury my sweet sister
    With a stone at her foot and her head,
And ye must cover her fair body
    With the white roses and red.

' And I must out to the greenwood,
    The roof shall never shelter me ;
And I shall lie for seven long years
    On the grass below the hawthorn tree.'

HELIODORE.

(MELEAGER.)

POUR wine, and cry again, again, again!
   To Heliodore!
And mingle the sweet word ye call in vain
   With that ye pour!
And bring to me her wreath of yesterday
   That's dank with myrrh;
Hesternæ Rosæ, ah my friends, but they
   Remember her!
Lo the kind roses, loved of lovers, weep
   As who repine,
For if on any breast they see her sleep
   It is not mine!

THE PROPHET.

(ANTIPHILUS.)

I KNEW it in your childish grace
    The dawning of Desire,
'Who lives,' I said, 'will see that face
    Set all the world on fire!'
They mocked; but Time has brought to pass
    The saying over-true;
Prophet and martyr now, alas,
    I burn for Truth,—and you!

LAIS.

(POMPEIUS.)

LAIS that bloomed for all the world's delight,
    Crowned with all love lilies, the fair and dear,
Sleeps the predestined sleep, nor knows the flight
    Of Helios, the gold-reined charioteer:
Revel, and kiss, and love, and hate, one Night
    Darkens, that never lamp of Love may cheer!

CLEARISTA.

(MELEAGER.)

FOR Death, not for Love, hast thou
    Loosened thy zone!
Flutes filled thy bower but now,
    Morning brings moan!
Maids round thy bridal bed
    Hushed are in gloom,
Torches to Love that led
    Light to the tomb!

THE FISHERMAN'S TOMB.

(LEONIDAS OF TARENTUM.)

THERIS the Old, the waves that harvested
   More keen than birds that labour in the sea,
With spear and net, by shore and rocky bed,
   Not with the well-manned galley laboured he;
Him not the star of storms, nor sudden sweep
   Of wind with all his years hath smitten and bent,
But in his hut of reeds he fell asleep,
   As fades a lamp when all the oil is spent:
This tomb nor wife nor children raised, but we
His fellow-toilers, fishers of the sea.

OF HIS DEATH.

(MELEAGER.)

AH Love, my Master, hear me swear
By all the locks of Timo's hair,
By Demo, and that fragrant spell
Wherewith her body doth enchant
Such dreams as drowsy lovers haunt,
By Ilias' mirth delectable.
And by the lamp that sheds his light
On love and lovers all the night,
By those, ah Love, I swear that thou
Hast left me but one breath, and now
Upon my lips it fluttereth,
Yet *this* I'll yield, my latest breath,
Even this, oh Love, for thee to Death !

RHODOPE.

(RUFINUS.)

THOU hast Hera's eyes, thou hast Pallas' hands,
And the feet of the Queen of the yellow sands,
Thou hast beautiful Aphrodite's breast,
Thou art made of each goddess's loveliest !
Happy is he who sees thy face,
Happy who hears thy words of grace,
And he that shall kiss thee is half divine,
But a god who shall win that heart of thine !

TO A GIRL.

(ASCLEPIADES.)

BELIEVE me, love, it is not good
    To hoard a mortal maidenhood ;
In Hades thou wilt never find,
Maiden, a lover to thy mind ;
Love 's for the living ! presently
Ashes and dust in death are we !

TO THE SHIPS.

(MELEAGER.)

O GENTLE ships that skim the seas,
   And cleave the strait where Hellé fell,
Catch in your sails the Northern breeze,
   And speed to Cos, where she doth dwell,
   My Love, and see you greet her well!
And if she looks across the blue,
Speak, gentle ships, and tell her true,
' He comes, for Love hath brought him back,
No sailor, on the landward tack.'

If thus, oh gentle ships, ye do,
   Then may ye win the fairest gales,
And swifter speed across the blue,
   While Zeus breathes friendly on your sails.

A LATE CONVERT.

(PAULUS SILENTIARIUS.)

I THAT in youth had never been
   The servant of the Paphian Queen,
I that in youth had never felt
The shafts of Eros pierce and melt,
Cypris ! in later age, half grey,
I bow the neck to *thee* to-day.
Pallas, that was my lady, thou
Dost more triumphant vanquish now,
Than when thou gained'st, over seas,
The apple of the Hesperides.

THE LIMIT OF LIFE.

THIRTY-SIX is the term that the prophets assign,
And the students of stars to the years that are mine;
Nay, let thirty suffice, for the man who hath passed
Thirty years is a Nestor, and *he* died at last!

TO DANIEL ELZEVIR.

(FROM THE LATIN OF MÉNAGE.)

WHAT do I see! Oh gods divine
     And goddesses,—this Book of mine,—
This child of many hopes and fears,—
Is published by the Elzevirs!
Oh perfect Publishers complete!
Oh dainty volume, new and neat!
The Paper doth outshine the snow,
The Print is blacker than the crow,
The Title-Page, with crimson bright,
The vellum cover smooth and white,
All sorts of readers do invite,
Ay, and will keep them reading still,
Against their will, or with their will!
Thus what of grace the Rhymes may lack
The Publisher has given them back,
As Milliners adorn the fair
Whose charms are something skimp and spare.

Oh *dulce decus*, Elzevirs !
The pride of dead and dawning years,
How can a poet best repay
The debt he owes your House to-day?
May this round world, while aught endures,
Applaud, and buy, these books of yours !
May purchasers incessant pop,
My Elzevirs, within your shop,
And learned bards salute, with cheers,
The volumes of the Elzevirs,
Till your renown fills earth and sky,
Till men forget the Stephani,
And all that Aldus wrought, and all
Turnebus sold in shop or stall,
While still may Fate's (and Binders') shears
Respect, and spare, the Elzevirs !

THE LAST CHANCE

THE LAST CHANCE.

WITHIN the streams, Pausanias saith,
    That down Cocytus valley flow,
Girdling the grey domain of Death,
    The spectral fishes come and go ;
The ghosts of trout flit to and fro.
    Persephone, fulfil my wish,
And grant that in the shades below
    My ghost may land the ghosts of fish.

Φῆ λογοποιὸς ἀνήρ, δνοφερῶν ἔντοσθε ῥεέθρων
    ὅσσα πέριξ Ἀιδην εἰς Ἀχέροντα ῥέει
ἰχθύες ὡς ἂν᾽ ἀφεγγὲς ὕδωρ σκιαὶ ἀΐσσουσιν
    εἴδωλ᾽ εἰδώλοις νηχόμενα πτερύγων.
Φερσεφόνη, σὺ θανόντι δ᾽ ἐμοὶ κρήηνον ἐέλδωρ,
    κἂν Ἀιδῃ σκιεροὺς ἰχθύας ἐξερύσαι.
L. C.

www.ingramcontent.com/pod-product-compliance
Lightning Source LLC
Chambersburg PA
CBHW030353170426
43202CB00010B/1363